Dunhurst

Witches of Dorset

GW00685228

RODNEY LEGG
and
OLIVE KNOTT

DORSET PUBLISHING COMAPNY
at the WINCANTON PRESS
NATIONAL SCHOOL, NORTH STREET
WINCANTON, SOMERSET BA9 9AT

THE OCCULT IS INSEPARABLE FROM THE DOWNLANDS OF WESSEX.
WILLIAM BLAKE'S ENGRAVING 'THE SERPENT TEMPLE'.

Contents

PUBLISHING DETAILS: Second edition, 1996. Copyright Dorset Publishing Comapnay © 1974, being originally based on passages from **Witches of Wessex** and **Down Dorset Way** which were assigned to Rodney Legg by Olive Knott on 3 February 1974 and rewritten and extended by him, in colabortaion with Amanda Allsop, into this present edition. All rights reserved. Printed by Wincanton Press and distrubuted by Westcountry Books, from Halsgrove House, Lower Moor Way, Tiverton, Devon EX16 6SS. Telephone 01-884-243-242

International standard book number ISBN 0 948699 54 X

WARNING TO READERS: This is intended as a book of folklore and an investigation into one of the lesser known aspects of the history of the Dorset countryside. Because of its title, however, there is a chance that it may be bought by people who feel oppressed by the black arts.

They must realise that the power of witchcraft has never rested with witches but lies in the minds of its victims. The commonplace proof of this statement has been provided by mediums and spiritualists. For if a medium is sufficiently criminally insane to predict a date of death to a person then that client's death will probably prove to have been forecast correctly. But if the same message had been given to a third party, and not imparted to the person concerned, then it would not have come true.

Individuals can scare themselves to death. Fear, and not occult influences, will have been their killer. The power of witchcraft rests in the belief of its victims.

The witch in literature. Aubrey Beardsley's well known drawing of one of the arch-witches from Sir Thomas Malory's "Le Morte D'Arthur." Another Beardsley drawing is on page six.

Introducing the witch cult

WITCHCRAFT is still without doubt an underground cult in the English countryside but this little book concerns the old school of witches and the deeper beliefs which survived in Dorset into living memory. It is the first time a book has been devoted exclusively to the **Witches of Dorset** and has grown out of my own **Witches of Wessex** which was published in 1961 and went out of print a long time ago. The idea for that came from the late Captain George Pitt-Rivers of the Manor House at Hinton St. Mary, who casually told me one day: "You should write a book about witches."

When the original edition was published he wrote to me: "I feel certain that you must have enjoyed your research work particularly in this area, as you must be acquainted with Margaret Murray's book 'Witchcult in Western Europe' where she describes the covens that are still to be found in parts of Cornwall, Devon and Dorset. I believe that our last qualified witch of Farnham, on Cranborne Chase, was much skilled in giving the evil eye and hanging up bottles containing certain potions in the chimney."

Much of the fieldwork for the earlier book was carried out by Richard Ryder of Rempstone in Purbeck. This time Rodney Legg has provided the history of the Dorset mizmazes, and together with Amanda Allsop collected a number of documentary accounts of witchcraft in Victorian times and earlier. As before, I have taken a particular pleasure in obtaining stories by word of mouth from local men and women who tell them with great relish, if at the same time with tongue in cheek. It is noticeable that most of the tales follow a traditional pattern and belong to the ancient folklore not only of Dorset but of the whole of England.

The Dorset Ooser (pronounced 'osser'), for years in the hands of the Cave family at Holt Farm, Melbury Osmond, vanished in 1897. With bull horns, rounded boss on the forehead, wild bulging eyes, and lumped nose it is basic, animal and savage. It can only be the face of the devil. And that this horned mask had a place in active ceremonial cannot be disputed as the gnashing teeth were hinged with string and the face was obviously not made for static display.

Stephen Dewar writes that Melbury villagers recalled how it was brought out from its 'tallet' (hayloft) resting place and paraded with chains attached and "lucifer matches pushed alight into the head"—a skull-cap of crisped hair. "One is tempted to visualise smoke pouring from the infernal nostrils," he commented.

Tom Lethbridge, one of this century's greatest thinking archaeologists, noticed the bull was absent from pagan Saxon ornamental art. Bulls go back to Romano-British days, Mithraic ritual, and have left little mark in our surviving threadwork of ghost lore and superstition.

Only slight imagination is needed to see how the Ooser performed. The mediaeval witch trials provide abundant evidence that the devil "took the place of a kind of stud-bull in relation to the women of his particular coven or group of covens" and for this exhausting task he summoned the aid of an artificial phallus. This horned mask from Melbury was stolen and Lethbridge hoped it had gone back to its past: "One feels that it may have returned to some hidden coven in the area."

Ooser has been explained as a dialect survival of the Old English word **wuduwasa,** meaning satyr, curtailed by the tendency in Dorset speech for the loss of any initial 'w'—such as in 'woman' which becomes 'ooman.' Oser is also the 17th century Italian word for the devil of the Christian church.

Witches were tolerated for the first thousand years of Christian superiority. It is only fair to deduce, perhaps cynically, from the evidence of the vicious and murderous history of Christian intolerance that it must have taken this long before the church had sufficient confidence and superiority to unleash death on the followers of the old religion. Witchcraft was denounced as heresy by Pope Innocent III in 1484 and persecution continued till 1750. Conviction for the crime of witchcraft became a capital offence in Britain in 1563 and some 5,000 were executed in the British Isles, more than

The Ooser was the stud-bull of Dorset witchcraft and its Victorian discoverers stayed mum if they realised they were handling one of the most remarkable occult survivals ever found in this country. This mask would have been worn by the head of the coven and it was through him that the female members made intercourse with the devil. He penetrated them from behind with an artificial phallus. In olden accounts of the witch cult, the devil's penis is described as abnormally large, and his sperm is always said to be cold. The devil's disciples found their master more satisfying than any man. Tom Lethbridge suggests that the theft of the Ooser in 1897 may have marked its return to a west Dorset coven. The Ooser preserved as a museum piece would have been commendable, but it is far more exciting to think that he may still perform.

4,000 of them in Scotland, as a result of the Bible's words: "Thou shalt not suffer a witch to live."

They had few qualms in being martyred for their faith, preferred fire as the perfect death, and freely admitted "ritual dancing, sacred feasts, sexual licence and the working of harmful magic." But as Lethbridge says in his book 'Witches': "They never said, however, what their beliefs were, nor in whose honour their rites were performed."

These go back to the Mother Goddess, fertility and the dancing in the stone circles of the downs and western moors to ensure the continued synchronism of the sun and moon in their celestial paths. Some of their basic ideas, as with those of the Christians, were displaced by the heresy of knowledge—and the witches of today are left with the magic of the Underworld. Rudyard Kipling was right about their original purpose: "Oh, do not tell the priest our plight, or he would call it a sin; but we have been out in the woods all night a conjuring summer in." For us in Dorset the memory is still alive in a wealth of folk tales.

Their colourful imagery and poetic fancy alone are worth recording before the last of the witches jumps on her broomstick and flies away. It is easy to see how, at the beginning of this century, many an old woman was dubbed a witch. In the first place it may only have been that her behaviour generally coincided with a somewhat strange appearance. Then, if she made some wild prophecy which happened to come true, her reputation would grow until belief in her evil powers made her feared by all with whom she came into contact, and established her as a witch.

This belief was never more strong than in the outlying villages and hamlets of the Dorset of Thomas Hardy's day. Many a farm labourer after a day of toil from dawn to sunset would go miles out of his way rather than pass a witch's dwelling in the dark. More educated people, too, often shared this fear. A doctor is known to have said that he would not dare to ride through Henstridge on his bicycle lest the evil eye of a witch should bring misfortune upon him.

The Christians follow the foul biblical edict: "Thou shalt not suffer a witch to live." This woodcut showing the execution of witches is from Ralph Gardiner's strangely titled book, "England's Grievance Discovered in Relation to the Coal Trade," which was published in 1655.

A rector of Blandford is reputed to have instructed his maids that a certain woman who called at his house was never to leave the place empty handed.

A difficulty of transport no doubt fostered these crude beliefs for there were many who rarely passed the confines of their village during a life-time. A woman who lived two miles from Blandford had never been into the town, and had, in fact, for eighteen years refused to go outside her door. She considered herself bewitched although the person with the baleful eye had long since passed away.

It is not surprising that various methods were used to counteract the evil influence of witches so charms were called into being and visits to a 'white witch' or 'cunning man' frequently made. Bullocks' hearts stuffed with pins were placed in the wide chimneys to circumvent the entry of a witch. A horseshoe was hung over the cottage doorways to break the spell of the evil-wisher, and most barbaric of all methods to counteract evil spells was the crucifixion of a live animal in the roof.

Evidence of this practice may be seen today in the Coventry Arms, Corfe Mullen, an ancient building once a coaching inn on the main turnpike road from London to Dorchester.

Here, in a glass case overhanging the bar, may be seen the mummified body of a cat, which had been nailed to the rafters. It was during the process of alterations to the house that the remains of the animal were discovered. The pinioned form of the carcase is unmistakable evidence of the fate of the unfortunate creature said to have been used in the performance of black magic rites, possibly three hundred years ago. Another case of a mummified cat, at Blandford, is discussed later in this book.

Perhaps the most popular remedy of all was the drawing of the witch's blood unseen by her.

The latest case of cutting for this purpose, was at Charlton Marshall in 1939. Here the evil-wisher was a man who frequented the local inn. Bad luck or illness for some reason had been attributed to him. One evening, when the man was quietly drinking his first

---

Opposite: Sadism was an art form in Christian Europe and developed its own rituals in which death was painfully postponed for as long as the victims could withstand. At first the Pope slayed the members of the Cathar sect in the south of France because they followed wayward Christian beliefs. Then he accused them of conspiracy with the devil. This started the persecution of witches.

pint of ale, he was surreptitiously cut on the hand and arm by one who considered himself a sufferer from his overlooking.

Even backwardness in children was attributed to the power of witchcraft and quite recently the father of a slow-witted child consulted a white witch living at Bournemouth and was told, "Everything will be all right from now on." Strangely enough, that night, the evil-wisher died.

Similarly, only a few years ago a man living in Blandford who was a chronic invalid believed himself to be overlooked by a reputed witch. Her shadow on the sun-blind was sufficient to cause a relapse and it was just after seeing this shadow, the old man died.

It was quite a common belief that witches took other shapes. These were thought to be frogs, toads, and more frequently hares. It was believed that a witch masquerading as a hare could be killed if a silver coin was used as a bullet. Thus the story goes that in the village of Thorncombe there lived a witch who was the cause of much sickness and trouble in the district.

One of the villagers on his way home from work saw a hare, and firmly believing that here at hand was the over-looker, took aim with his gun, but missed it. Nothing daunted, he went home, found a silver three-penny bit and put it in front of the charge. Then carrying the gun with him till he saw the hare again, he took aim once more. This time he was successful.

He took it home, skinned it, and put it in the stew-pot to cook. Strange to relate, the pot cracked.

This belief in familiars is by no means confined to the west of England, for, even today in many parts of Africa, a belief in witchcraft sorcery is still very strong. Anyone having the ability to kill by secret and unnatural means is termed a 'witch doctor'. These witch doctors are thought to be able to turn themselves into animals to perform their dark deeds, and in these forms they must kill and live on human beings in order that the witch doctor himself may remain alive.

The equipment of the latter vies with many attributes of the witches in Hans Andersen's fairy tales for the witch doctor of Africa carries with him beside his

'Kalilosi' gun with magical powers, "human skulls, the partial skeleton of an African baby, a jar of human fat, weird little dancing dolls, diviners' bowls, rattles containing human bones, leather head-dresses and animal-skin costumes and animals' tails by which the owner claims to direct the lightning."

The dancing dolls are weird little statues ornamented with leather and are made to dance by the witch doctor and to cast evil spells upon his enemies.

This fear in the power of witchcraft is so strong that only a few years ago, an African was exonerated by the High Court at Port Herald, Nyasaland, for killing a witch. He believed the death of his brother had been brought about by a cousin who was a witch. He had shot her in the stomach with an arrow and hit her on the head with a hoe.

There is some attempt, however, by the natives themselves, to stamp out this evil. A group calling themselves the "Society of Twelve" have built temples to which they invite witch doctors "to turn over the tools of their practice and become cleansed."

The religious teaching and education of the mission schools is, of course, doing much to dispel these fears caused by lack of knowledge.

Another section makes a religion of the performance of the ancient rites of witchcraft and hold their meetings in a sixteenth century cottage which they call their temple and give the name of high priest to their leader. They have registered the cottage as a religious house and here they meet to worship the goddess of fertility. They dance in the nude around the altar, burning incense to the life-force which they have made a deity.

The group registers about four hundred and claims to be intellectual. Apparently it is difficult to qualify as a member and a good deal of probing into the background of would-be candidates is done.

Their object is entirely retrogressive. They claim to follow pagan rites which existed in Britain before Christianity. This belief in witchcraft, the origin of which ⁓eems to coincide with that of the human race, has been in evidence since biblical times, when the witch of Endor is said to have called up the spirit of Samuel and the

Matthew Hopkins, the dreaded Witchfinder General of this 1647 print, operated with Cromwell's blessing in Puritan areas of Civil War England. He accused and hanged hundreds of unfortunate people.

people of God were warned against her power.

In this country the burning and drowning of witches was at its height during the seventeenth century. A woman believed to be a witch, often by heredity, was subjected to the ordeal by water, that is, her hands and feet were tied together with ropes and she was lowered into the water. If by some fluke she floated, which sometimes happened by reason of her voluminous skirts buoying her up, this was thought to be a revelation of God and the victim was released from the bondage of the ropes and burnt at the stake. If, as was more often the case, the poor creature sank to the bottom and was drowned, the ignorant crowd accepted this as an equally just punishment for the appearance of evil.

It was in the eighteenth century that the last case of hanging for witchcraft in this country was registered. A certain Mary Hicks and her daughter, aged eleven, both self-confessed witches were accused of having rolled a stocking into a lather of soap and by so doing causing a ship to sink. They were condemned to death and were hanged at Huntingdon in 1716.

In 1971. a vicar in a parish on the edge of Dorset's Marshwood Vale was reluctant to talk about witchcraft as "he did not want to get the wrong side of the witches." Advertising a seven-toed cat in our regional rural newspaper is enough to bring every witch from Dorset and Somerset to your doorstep. A down-to-earth west Dorset doctor will testify to cases of the mysterious. healing of farm animals brought about by witches. Several of these are reputed in the Marshwood Vale alone but no one will talk about them. So this book has, regretfully, to be about Dorset's witches of yesteryear.

John Walsh
of Netherbury

ONE OF THE earliest cases of witchcraft in Dorset has
as its victim John Walsh of Netherbury near Beaminster
who faced trial in 1561. His case has been investigated
by Mr. Henry Bartlett of Shipton Gorge, near Bridport,
who sent his findings to the Dorset Evening Echo in
1963. Walsh was said to have "consorted with white,
green and black fairies who were cavorting on the hills
of Dorset."

The devil, said Walsh, "had a cloven hoof, and
personally asked him to give a drip of blood each year
—and a gift of two living things. Cats, dogs, and chickens
were the devil's desire."

No details survive of the poor man's fate but it
seems clear he was cruelly tortured into making his
confessions.

In the past hundred years there have occasionally
been reminders that witchcraft is not totally forgotten
in the isolated farmsteads and hamlets of the Marshwood
Vale. Deep in the hills that skirt the Vale's western
edge, in 1884 at a house in Hawkchurch on the Devon
border, an obstruction was found lodged in the chimney.
The building had been recently vacated by its tenant:

"The obstruction was got out, and was found to be
neither brick nor stone, but a bullock's heart, with which
stuck a quantity of the prickles of the white thorn,
some nails, pins and other things."

A villager suggested that the former occupier, a
bachelor, had possibly used the charm "to ward off the
attacks of the ladies" and to prevent 'witches' from
gaining access to the house via the chimney.

The previous year, 1883, an amazing story was re-
ported from the countryside near Bridport. A dairyman's
wife was induced by two 'strange women'—probably
gipsies—into believing that money could literally 'breed'
money. The gullible housewife gave them some
sovereigns which the two women pretended to seal in a
charmed sheep's heart with the warning that the heart

was to remain secreted and unopened until Easter Sunday.

But the dairyman missed his money long before then, and the wife had to tell him that it was hidden away for a reason. He found in the chimney a smoked sheep's heart studded with pins in mystic patterns. Inside the heart were some bright, shining farthings.

Perhaps the superstitious would have said that the turning of the sovereigns into farthings was the penalty for breaking the spell. His wife believed they would have discovered "quite a happy family of new sovereigns and young half-sovereigns." Certainly, the two unknown women vanished the richer by several pounds.

As Reverend R. F. Meredith, rector of the west Dorset parish of Halstock, wrote to The Times in 1883: "There is no need to go to west Prussia for witchcraft. In a parish where the counties of Devon, Dorset and Somerset meet, a young man, being afflicted with scrofula which caused at times contraction of the muscles of the right thigh and very considerable pain, formed the idea that a poor delicate woman living next door, wife of a labourer and mother of several children, had bewitched him, and one day in his agony rushed into her house with a sewing needle, and before the woman had time to think, scratched her severely in the neck and in four places on her bare arm, drawing blood in each instance, then rubbed his hand on the blood and ran off. The poor woman came to me to complain, showing the scratches, and I advised her to take out a summons before the justices, but time passed. The young man, as usual, felt relieved of his pains for a time, and his mother, a widow occupying a few acres of land with her cows and pigs, tried to assure me that drawing the blood cured her son, for she considered the other woman had 'overlooked' him!"

Belief in witchcraft was widespread throughout west Dorset in the closing years of Victoria's reign. In 1884 the Bridport News gave the case of a woman, the wife of a woodman living in a parish towards Dorchester, who had been seriously ill for a long time. This woman was treated by a gipsy who told her she had been 'overlooked'.

The gipsy also informed her that she would never recover until the spell had been broken—something she said she could do for a small sum of money. The sick woman readily agreed and paid. She was then instructed by the gipsy to place certain flowerpots out of doors; when the flowers withered she would mend. The woman implicitly followed these and other instructions, and she recovered, as predicted, when the flowers drooped.

Opposite: Puritans from England took their brutal intolerances across the Atlantic to the British colonies on the American seaboard. This print shows one of their twenty victims at Salem, New England, in 1692. She is Bridget Bishop and she met her death on Gallows Hill.

Deanes Gimmerton
of Lyme Regis

A SEVENTEENTH CENTURY case of witchcraft in Dorset occurred at Lyme Regis where, on 1 June 1687, Deanes Gimmerton, a local housewife, was tried on several charges of 'bewitching' her young neighbours.

The case was brought by Richard Scorch, whose eighteen-year-old son Nathaniel had become ill the previous April after smoking tobacco from a pipe which Deanes Gimmerton had prepared, and offered him. At first he suffered only weakness and general debilitation. On 23 May, he was taken with a violent fit lasting two hours—six people were needed to hold him down in his bed. The fits continued and grew stronger.

Whenever he was taken with one of his fits, Nathaniel saw the apparition of Deanes Gimmerton. After several of these violent sessions, several pins and one iron nail were discovered in various parts of his body. Deanes always appeared to him at the same spot in the room; and when his family struck at the spot he indicated, his pain only increased, so that he begged them not to do anything. He remained weak and "in a pining and languishing condition."

Another witness was Mary Tillman, whose daughter Elizabeth was taken ill in the same way in 1682, when she too was eighteen. She had the same fits and also saw the apparition of Deanes Gimmerton. Brass pins were found on her body, and when her family tried to destroy them, Elizabeth's pain increased. In one of her fits, she was unable to move over from the stool where she was sitting, to her bed, and she said that Deanes Gimmerton kept her there. No one could move her.

Elizabeth languished, with periodic fits, for three years, and finally died. Two days before she died a neighbour visited her and asked her how she was. She replied that she could not speak about her condition because Deanes Gimmerton was sitting on her bed.

The outcome of Deanes Gimmerton's trial is not known.

Johane Guppie
of South Perrott

AMID ALL the persecution of so-called witches in the seventeenth century, there was one victim in a west Dorset parish who inspired a whole community to rise to her defence. The people of South Perrott were anxious to lay the potentially fatal rumours about Johane Guppie and banded together to issue the following statement which is set out here with its original spellings of the time:

"To all Christian people to whome this present certificate shall come wee the parishioners of South Perrott in the county of Dorset where Johane Guppie, the wiefe of Thomas Guppie, nowe dwelleth and of Stoke Abbott where the said Johane was born and of other parishes neere theer aboutes whose names are hereunder writen send greetinge in our Lord God. Know ye that wee the said parishioners and inhabitantes of the said places and thereabouts doe by theeis presentes signifie affirme and declare that the said Johane Guppie during all the time of her aboade and dwellinge in South Perrott aforesaid and before her coming theer hath did and doth behave herself in all things well and honestlye and never did to our knowledges or as we have ever heard eyther hurte or damage to anye person or persons whatsoever by waye of enchantmente sorcerye or witchcraft nor was ever accompted reckoned or knowen to be a woman that ever could use anye such thinge or to be a woman of the sorte condition or qualitie but contrariwise she hath donne good manye people aswell in curinge of dyvers peoples wounds and such like thinges as in drenchinge of cattell and such like exercises and alwayes hath lyved of good name and fame without anye spott or touch of enchantmente sorcerye or witchcraft. All which wee the parties hereunder named and menconed shall and wilbe alwayes readye to affirme and maynteyne whersoever and when wee shalbe called thereunto."

There follow the signatures of over twenty people.

Bewitched boats
of Abbotsbury

HOLY STONES, or witch-stones as they are called, are those beach pebbles with a natural hole in the centre. They are also known as hag-stones and were often tied to a door-key and carried around as a precaution against witches and evil spirits. Others would tie them to the cast-iron bedhead. Again, the combination of a holy stone and iron was a powerful preventive measure.

In Dorset, in the late 1830s and -40s, it was not uncommon to see such stones dangling from the large open rowing boats at Weymouth. They would hang from nails or staples close beneath the gunwale, the upper edge of timber running round the boat's side. In this way the stones could be used in conjunction with iron.

Sometimes, at Abbotsbury, a boat would fail to catch any fish even though there might be great shoals all around and the other boats in the party would be hauling full nets on to the Chesil Bank. The unlucky boat would be considered bewitched. And the only way this spell could be broken was to attach a mackerel, liberally stuck with pins, to the rudder.

Abbotsbury's annual pagan survival was Garland Day on 13 May when flower-covered structures were carried on poles around the village and then on to the beach where, in shades of the fertility cult, games and festivities took place. All the village took part and the garlands were finally placed in the fishing boats and taken out to sea where they were cast overboard to drift on the waves.

Inland, other methods of witch-prevention were used. Ralph Wightman gave a traditional Dorset method of avoiding being overlooked by the evil eye when he took part in a "Country Questions" broadcast on 24 May, 1964. Tie a knot of Mountain Ash into a cross, he said, and then thread this into the hairs of a cow's tail.

Witches Corner
at Leigh

MAZES ARE AMONG the most obscure earthworks in the field of British archaeology, having parallels in the Cretan and Egyptian labyrinths, and probably marking the sites of prehistoric dancing grounds. They are inextricably bound up with the rituals of life, death and fertility in the ages when the Celtic paganism of the old religion held sway in these islands. Like Christmas and the other fixed festivals of Christianity, mazes were a symbol of the past so strong that adoption instead of suppression was the method by which their power could be transferred and assimilated into the thought processes of Christ's millennium. Mazes were set in the floors of cathedrals in Italy and France.

In England, a handful of what are probably genuine prehistoric mazes have survived in a Celtic setting. On the open downland of Cranborne Chase, at Breamore Down near Whitsbury, a maze with shallow ditches separated by grassy banks lies on a ridge surrounded by Iron Age field systems. Likewise, the now ploughed maze at Pimperne near Blandford is in an area marked by the lines and depressions of intensive prehistoric occupation and farming. Another lies inside the Iron Age fort of St. Catherine's Hill at Winchester.

The immediate environs of Dorchester contain placenames which give clues to those who wish to trace its distant past. As in Ireland, where the so-called "pleasant hills" have been defined as "ceremonial hills," the Mount Pleasant near Thomas Hardy's Max Gate home has been confirmed by excavation as a Bronze Age sacred circle. On the chalk slopes on the other side of the Frome, is a small collection of farm buildings and cottages beside the main road to Puddletown. It is known as Troy Town.

Mazes are often known at "Troytowns" and Virgil described the "game of Troy" played as in Crete where "the labyrinth of old between blind walls its secret hid from view." So-called "Troy games" were performed by the young men of the royal household of Edward II in their military ride and tournament held on every Sunday in Lent.

Witches and fairies, too, are remembered in conjunction with mazes—"the yellow skirted fays, fly after the night steeds, leaving their moon-loved maze."

Here, from the depths of the Blackmore Vale in a pasture at Leigh near Yetminster, Dorset provides oral tradition and documentary evidence that connects a maze with witchcraft. The Mizmaze at Leigh is about a third of a mile south of the village church and today consists of a hexagonal bank about 75 feet across, enclosing a raised circular platform in the middle which used to be marked with turf-cut paths. These, according to Thomas Gerrard in the 1620s, were re-cut once a year and repaired by the young men of the village. A ditch runs around the outside of the Mizmaze.

Though only standing at 300 feet above sea level in the heart of the Vale claylands, the Mizmaze is positioned at the top of a low, rounded hill between Back Drove and Leigh Village. From its banks there is open visibility for many miles over the countryside around, to the ridge above Sherborne, and in the other direction to the chalk downs at High Stoy.

William Barnes recorded the traditions of the Leigh Mizmaze in a paper he presented to the Dorset Field Club in 1879: "Many years ago I was told by a man of this neighbourhood that a corner of Leigh Common was called 'Witches Corner'; and long again after that a friend gave me some old depositions on witchcraft taken before Somerset magistrates from about the years 1650 to 1664. The cases were of Somerset, and touched in some points Dorsetshire; and the one of the witches' sisterhood said that they sometimes met in Leigh Common. This proof of the meeting of witches in Leigh Common as the ground of the traditional name of 'witches corner' is interesting as a token of truth in tradition."

Apparently from these depositions, Barnes described the evil spells worked by the witches on those they intended to bewitch. They made a waxen image in the likeness of the person they wished to injure and with 'Christian' ceremonial gave it a name. Having done this they pricked the image with pins causing the unfortunate individual represented to suffer the pangs of "thorns in the flesh."

They danced and chanted around the representation of their victim evoking a deadly incantation. Then at length, having indulged in these sadistic revellings they placed the image before a fire already kindled and as it melted, willed its counterpart to pine away.

Perhaps, with the geographical closeness of the Mizmaze, these allegations amount to the exposure of a genuine witch coven and are more than just another purge carried out during the witch-hunting hysteria which swept the countryside of Puritan England in the dark days that followed the Civil War.

Jenny Andrews of Beaminster

AN OLD winding lane leads from the main road at Beaminster Down across Horn Hill and towards Broadwindsor. About midway the track dips into a hollow and here by a pond known as Frog's Pool once stood a lonely thatched cottage. The setting was perfect for black magic and it is not surprising that the old woman who lived there was dubbed a witch.

Children half repelled, yet half attracted, would hurry by the cottage in daylight glancing back over their shoulders for a possible glimpse of Old Jenny with her black dress and apron and her bonnet tied under her chin. After dark they would not venture down the lane at all for it was said that the witch took frogs from the pond and with them brewed her charms and spells.

Old Jenny was a by-word in the neighbourhood and when children annoyed their parents the latter would cry: "I'll send Jenny after 'ee," or "Jenny'll 'ave thee, sure enough."

In time, the old woman's powers became legendary. There is a story told that one day a man was passing Frog Pool Cottage with a load of coal which had already been commissioned when Jenny came out and demanded a hundred-weight from his load.

"No," said the man, "this is all bespoke."

"Then," said the witch, stepping into the lane with fist up-raised, "thic hoss oon't move out o' this lane till I get my coal."

And sure enough, like Baalam's Ass, the horse stood still. No proddings or cracks from the whip, no inducement such as "Woak-off, there, Prince" would make the animal move an inch. Had the horse seen a vision of ten thousand armed men barring the way with flaming swords he could not have been more adamant.

Yet Jenny, it seems, did nothing but look at the horse and—look at the horse.

The driver, having no alternative but to spend eternity in the lane with a load of undelivered coal, reluctantly dropped a bag at Jenny's feet. Prince, as if released from some petrifying agency, was suddenly galvanised into action, and proceeded on his way to Broadwindsor without word from driver or witch.

Sarah Smith
of Sherborne

PUBLIC INTEREST in the Sherborne petty sessions of September 1884, was excited by a case arising out of alleged 'witchery' at Cold Harbour in the town's poor north-eastern quarter. The court was crowded with eager listeners who wanted to know the outcome of an incident on the 19th of that month.

Tamar Humphries, a married woman, was the defendant and she was accused of assault. The magistrates were told that she entered the garden of her next door neighbour, Sarah Smith—described as being "on the shady side of eighty"—and shook the old lady by her shoulders, saying: "Oh, Sal Smith, what's thee done to my child? You're a witch, and I'll draw the blood of thee."

Mrs Humphries held a stocking needle in her hand and with this weapon "she made free use about the complainant's hands and arms."

Sarah Smith, questioned by the defence, said she had been the Humphries' neighbour for thirty years and that they had never quarrelled before. Sidney Watts, the defending lawyer, could only plead for his client that she had heard Sarah Smith "give her a bad name" and claim that the violence used amounted only to "a gentle shake." The defendant was in an upset state because her daughter was crippled with rheumatism.

The Bench took a more serious view of the garden blood-letting and considered it amounted to a disgraceful assault on an inoffensive old woman, who happened to be digging potatoes at the time. So they fined Tamar Humphries £1 with 11s 6d costs which in those days was more than a token penalty.

Mommet
on the Borderland

THIS STORY comes from a few miles across the Dorset border. It is worth including here with the witch-lore of this county as the witches of the borderland invariably influenced a wide area and included customers and victims from the adjoining county. A Somerset farmer believed himself to be overlooked by an old couple in the village, since for some time he had had ill-luck with his cattle and crops.

Consequently he threatened the two old people, informed the police and the case was brought to court. The farmer's wife appeared on behalf of her husband and was asked the question: "Does your husband really believe that he has been bewitched by these people?" She answered: "Yes, he hung a mommet in a tree, but it didn't work."

The mommet was a stuffed rag doll, another form of the waxen image, which was supposed to represent the ill-wisher. Those who believed themselves to be overlooked would dig pins into the figure and eventually burn it. This they considered was effectual in breaking the spell of the evil-wisher.

The term mommet is still used in the West Country although its original use has completely died out. A mother annoyed with one of her children will call him a "mommet," but from this word like many which have been incorporated into everyday language the initial sting has been entirely removed.

Right: A witch preparing a potion—painted by an unknown master of the Flemish school in the mid-15th century.

Mother Weller
of Milborne Port

BY ALL ACCOUNTS Mother Weller of Milborne Port near Sherborne, more often waved the black stick than the magic wand. Clad in a long black skirt and cape and wearing, when out of doors, a little black toque which accentuated her ghastly white face, she looked with her piercing black eyes, a witch indeed. Added to this she had a peculiar high-stepping gait, not unlike a frog's jump and this was said to be on account of her taking the shape of a frog or toad at night.

Mother Weller lived in a lonely cottage on the edge of the downs. Apparently this was one of the pair that stood immediately south of Three Arch Bridge, beside the railway, a mile out of the village. It was the only building which lay near the hilltop lane that ran from Gainsborough to the old farmhouse on Milborne Down.

Children feared her and ran past her cottage with furtive backward glances. "High Steppin' Weller" they called her amongst themselves but did not dare to incur her wrath by shouting after her in the country roads.

She was believed to possess the evil eye which she placed mostly upon cattle, and pigs. Whole litters of pigs would sicken mysteriously and die, horses would go lame and cows go sick and all would be attributed to the 'over-looking' of Mother Weller's beady eye.

Horse-shoes placed over cottage doorways, hearts stuffed with pins pushed up the chimney were all of no avail to break the spell she wove. Something much more drastic was needed. A farmer, who had no doubt suffered from her 'evil eye', was considered instrumental in bringing about her death.

Believing, like many more in the neighbourhood that Mother Weller turned herself at night into an ugly toad the farmer, armed with a pitch fork, laid wait beside her cottage. His patience was rewarded when one evening, just at dusk, he saw a toad near the doorway of the witch's cottage. Without hesitation the man thrust the fork through the back of the toad.

Mother Weller was never seen again alive. She was found dead with a wound in her back. Even so, tradition says, the old woman's evil powers linger in the vicinity, especially at the three-arched railway bridge nearby. Here there have been several suicides and, strangely enough, here a young farmer was gored by a bull from the effects of which he shortly afterwards died.

Mother Herne
of Milborne Down

MENTION WITCHCRAFT to the older people at Milborne Port and they will think not of Mother Weller but of their memories of a far more widely-known lady. She was Mother Herne, of Milborne Down, who must take her place here as queen, amongst this conclave of witches. Her name will be remembered when lesser names of the sisterhood have long since been forgotten. People can still point to the spot in the hedgerow at the end of a narrow lane above Waterloo Crescent, where you come to the high-road crossing Milborne Down, and tell that it was here her cottage stood. On the map it is called Deadman's Hill.

It is now forty years since Mother Herne died but her picture is still vivid in my mind. I can see her bent little figure leaning over the cottage gate, her familiar—

a black cat—perched on her shoulder. She must have been quite eighty years old when I first met her but her hair, which was strained tightly back, was still raven-black, her skin was the colour of parchment and her eyes beady, black and penetrating to an alarming degree.

I first heard of Mother Herne, and the black art which she practised, when I used, in the company of other young girls, to hoe the flax which grew near her lonely cottage on the hills. We were employed by the neighbouring farmer and the blue of the flax rippling like waves of the sea is a sight I have never forgotten.

We were discussing her one day when we must have been a good mile from her cottage. The other girls had heard of her cures by the use of herbs and ointments, of the warts and toothaches she had charmed away, and how if you crossed her hand with silver she would foretell your future. I remember we investigated as to how much money we had, and discovered we could produce only a silver threepenny bit between us. However, we decided to venture and walked to her cottage and there was Mother Herne leaning over her gate. As if in anticipation of our visit, she called out in her cackling voice: "I baint gwaine t' tell 'ee yer fortunes fer nar threepenny bit."

Away we went, and it wasn't until much later that I summoned enough courage to pay her a visit accompanied by my sister. The appearance of her thatched cottage both inside and out would have made a suitable illustration for any child's fairy tale book. It might have been the 'sweet stuff' house, the home of the witch who entrapped Hansel and Gretel. It was a little four-roomed house with no fence around it, her black hens pecking at the grass round the door, a black goat tied to a nearby tree and Mother Herne, when she appeared, was again with her cat.

My sister and I were admitted to the interior of the cottage. The low ceiling was hung with bunches of herbs, a fire burnt on the open hearth and the room was filled with smoke.

There was a cauldron hung by a chain over the fire, and in that I suppose the witch brewed her charms and cures. I have since thought that Mother Herne did more good than harm, for she certainly put her strange powers to good purpose.

There was a settle by the fire and huddled into one corner of it was Mother Herne's third husband, for she had bewitched three men into sharing her strange existence. This one was aged like herself but palsied and infirm and to my excited imagination he seemed to be trying to warn us to take no heed of the woman's predictions. He was unable to articulate but his gestures and manners seemed to indicate his intention.

On entering the cottage the witch picked up a long carving knife which lay on the table and pointing it directly at my sister said "I've zid 'ee avore."

This remark, although innocent enough in itself, held somehow a sinister tinge and was enough to inspire my sister with terror, for Mother Herne had most certainly never seen her before.

Now the former moved to the cauldron and began stirring the mixture it contained muttering to herself the while and occasionally throwing something over her shoulder. Indeed the whole scene might have been the re-acting of some fairy tale which both fascinates and repels the children of all ages. There was an unexpected movement from the top of the settle giving us a turn; it was the cat which suddenly sprang on to the witch's shoulder.

At last Mother Herne gave us her attention. She came to me first and I gave her a silver coin. She held out her hand for me to cross it, and then after fixing me with her beady eye which somehow seemed to bore its way into my soul, she began tracing the lines on the palm of my hand with her long fingernail.

Then she told me my fortune and, unbelievable as it may sound, she made a faithful prediction of my future. She told my sister her fate, which also gradually worked itself out in afterlife.

I never visited Mother Herne again but I encountered her several times, on one occasion in a railway carriage. She was sitting there in the corner, her short legs dangling as they didn't reach the floor, and in her lap her wicker basket which she invariably carried on her visits to patients.

She occasionally visited sick people who were not

able to reach her cottage, taking with her the herbs and ointment necessary for the cures. These herbs, by the way, she gathered in the light of the full moon, thereby increasing their potency.

A friend was with me in the carriage. Presently two women got in and began discussing the witch of Milborne Down, whom they intended to visit, innocent of the fact that she was sitting opposite them.

"I wonder if we shall find the old bitch in?" they said. Mother Herne fixed her eye upon us, daring us to give away her presence. We were too frightened to speak but watched the little drama with a thrill of expectation.

However, nothing happened then but sometime after we again encountered Mother Herne on one of her expeditions and the witch came across the road to us and said "They vound th' old bitch in and they knowed it!" Then she gave her cackling laugh and we knew that she meant she had put something in their medicines which made them know they'd paid a visit to the cunning witch.

She was wise in more ways than one and realized that she could do more by reputation as a witch than as a herbalist. She knew so well how to practise her art, how to intimidate, or to inspire confidence as the case might be. Rich and poor alike believed in her power. Farmers visited her in secret when they believed their cattle to be overlooked. The wealthy invited her to their homes to cure their ailments and to give them advice when in trouble.

Her habitation was, to say the least, unsavoury. She kept cats and guinea-pigs, the latter in cages which were never cleaned out. Bunches of herbs hung from the roof and rats and mice ran freely about the room. From somewhere in the lower regions of her cottage would be heard a savage growling and the clanking of a chain. Mother Herne enjoyed the fear this inspired in her visitors and would say, "That's the divil down there. That's where I d'keep 'n."

Yet, there are many today who can testify to her cures. A man whose pig was ailing and refused to eat, sent his daughter to the cottage on the downs. Mother

Herne asked the exact whereabouts of the sty and in what way the pig was ailing, then closing her eyes, went into a kind of trance. On awakening she told the girl to go home and the animal would recover. When she reached her house the girl was informed that the pig was perfectly well and was eating its food.

A man suffering from acute toothache went in desperation to the Milborne witch. She took hold of his arm, looked up to the smoke-grimed ceiling and muttered a charm. The astounding thing about this cure was that the man never had toothache again. Mother Herne possessed, too, a strange power by which she could divine things happening unseen by her, or words spoken which she could not hear. A young woman once went to her for advice concerning the glove-making she was doing at the time. She took with her a friend and the pair wearing the long skirts of the day rode their bicycles. In order to keep their skirts from riding up it was the custom to strap the hem to the pedals. On nearing Ven House, which was some three miles from Mother Herne's cottage, the foot of one of the girls became entangled in the strap and she was nearly thrown off. She managed to save herself, however, and no serious damage was done.

When they reached the cottage, to their surprise, the witch greeted them with the words, "You had an accident on the way. Didn' hurt yerself, did 'ee? I know what you be come about, but don't 'ee worry; that'll come out all right." And sure enough it did. The young woman had been in some difficulty about her work which righted itself after the visit to Mother Herne.

On another occasion someone from Milborne Port went for help about her pig which persisted in jumping out of the sty, for all the world, she said, "as if he were bewitched."

"Bewitched, he is," said Mother Herne, "but you know the cure."

"Car on a brimble an' draw a drop o' blood." After she had scratched her evil wisher sufficiently to draw blood, her pig settled down in its sty.

Mother Herne was considered a white witch and able to charm away the evil effects of some lesser members of the sisterhood who practised the black art in the neighbourhood.

There was one story I heard about Mother Herne which was quite authentic as it was imparted to my mother by the doctor whom it concerned.

This doctor was Irish I remember and perhaps a little headstrong. He had had a patient suffering from boils in the neck which he was unable to cure. The former had gone to the witch for treatment and in a short time the boils had disappeared.

The doctor, then, his Irish temper roused, rode over in his pony and trap to vent his wrath on Mother Herne "Lay hands off my patient" he cried "or I'll have you put in Court."

"That's nothin' t' what I shall do t' thee," replied Mother Herne. "Think theeself lucky if thee's got home t' night wi' a broken neck." The doctor did not get home that night. He was found next day lying in a ditch with concussion of the brain, his horse dead beside him with a broken neck.

It was said that girls who had got themselves into trouble sought Mother Herne but she refused to help them out of their difficulties in any illegal way. One girl, however, she took into her cottage and cared for till her illegitimate child was born, showing that after all, Mother Herne hid a woman's heart beneath her witch's skin.

Her fame had spread for miles around. I have seen gigs and pony carts by the dozen lined up outside her cottage. She was visited by the local gentry, farmers' wives and people of all descriptions. Then people would come, in return for her cures and prophecies, to give her chicken, cheeses, home-baked bread, and cream. This was in addition to the silver by which they crossed her hand.

Mother Herne never paid rent for her cottage. It was more than the owner dared to ask—so I was not surprised to hear that when the old woman died she left a large sum of money.

As we should say today, "She had something." What it was is difficult to say, but she understood well the technique of the part she played in life. Her setting and atmosphere were perfect. Her appearance and personality went far to convince her public what they already half-wished to believe.

Good for Mother Herne that she made her entrance and her exit at the time she did. Had she appeared a century or two earlier she would undoubtedly have been either burnt at the stake or drowned. Today she would be regarded as a picturesque old relic of the past, a prey only to ignorance and superstition.

As an indication of the distance her fame spread I can give this example. Bernard Short, Poole's librarian and historian, who died in his eighties a few years ago, told Rodney Legg that in 1900 when he was sixteen, he was plagued by persistent warts on his hands. He heard of a middle-aged lady at Milborne Port who had mysterious healing powers, and cycled out to a quaint cottage deep in the countryside. She was a self-confessed white witch who confidently took his hands and told him the warts would vanish for ever. Within a week they had gone and would never return. The witch, who was almost certainly Mother Herne, also predicted his life would take a course far different from that which he intended, and could visualise him writing books about history, both of which were later to happen.

In 1973, in the post office at Milborne Port, an elderly gentleman told all he knew about Mother Herne: "One chap I remember, from Sherborne, had a birthmark deep red on his cheek and she got rid of that. She used to pick herbs when the moon was in a certain sphere, and give people the confidence they needed so that their toothaches and things would go away. I remember Bob Shepherd had toothache badly. 'You go on home, and don't you look behind,' she told him.

"He thought so much about not looking back that he forgot his teeth and they stopped hurting.

"She boiled up and strained herbs into good medicine. There wasn't any charge, but you were expected to give something. I've been out round there and passed by when there were up to six cars outside, so quite a few people had faith in her. The men who went there tried to keep it quiet, they didn't want it broadcast."

Old Mother Clinton of Stalbridge

OLD MOTHER CLINTON was established as the Stalbridge witch. Her cottage stood by a footpath which led to the bakehouse. The villagers went this way to the baker's shop when they took their cakes to be baked and the joints to be roasted. They rarely passed the cottage without going in for a little consultation with Mother Clinton. However, although she was held responsible for using the black stick and foretelling the future she was not infallible, for on one occasion two girls, already married, removed their wedding rings and in sceptical mood visited the Stalbridge witch.

"I know what you be thinkin' about," said Mother Clinton, to one of the girls.

"I bet you can't," the girl said.

"Oh yes, I can. You be thinkin' of that fair young man you'm goin' to marry."

"Well, now I'll tell 'ee what I'm thinkin'," said the girl, whose husband was dark. "I'm thinkin' you'm the biggest liar in Stalbridge."

So even at that time there were those who doubted.

The charming away of warts was by no means confined to the sisterhood. There were one or two men possessed of this art. One of these old men was met in the village by a girl who told him, "Marjie's got dree warts."

"Sure 'tis dree," said the old man. "Make 'em bleed an' they'll goo away.

"How be they warts?" he said to the girl when after a few days they met again. "Oh, they be gone," she said.

A mystery hung around the curing of warts and the method employed varied with each individual. On being asked what exactly it was which effected the cure the old man would say: "I d'blow 'em to the moon."

There was another old man in the area alleged to be able to cure toothache. A woman at Stalbridge tells the story that when a young girl she was suffering from toothache, she went to this man. As he talked to her the woman said, the toothache became easier and then ceased. "Now," he said, carefully folding a piece of paper into a true lover's knot, "Sew this into yer stays and never undo it, or you'll git toothache again."

The girl carried out his injunctions. She sewed the true lover's knot into her stays and when at length she needed some more, she removed it and sewed it into the new ones.

She married, the lover's knot still tied beneath her stays and she herself still free from the stabbing pain of toothache. But at length her curiosity getting the better of her she one day removed the charm from her stays, undid it and read the strange lettering inside. There were six letters only, the first letter of well known Bible verses. Having read them and disposed of the paper the woman was assailed by a violent attack of toothache.

The same woman, as a young girl was ailing and had every symptom of going into a decline. This time a cure was effected by a little old woman who went from door to door selling lace. She looked into the cottage and saw the girl lying on a couch. "Me dear," she said to the girl's mother, "You'll lose your daughter."

Going up to the girl she took her hand and said, "If you do what I tell 'ee, in three weeks you'll be cured."

"Get a dandelion root, some red docks which have growed on a dung mixen, some ground ivy, and some hay-maiden.

"Boil these to a syrup and take dree wine-glass fulls every day."

"Be sure," she said, "that the docks have a'growed on a dung mixen."

Her instructions were carefully carried out, the girl began to improve and at the end of three weeks was completely cured.

There was another old woman of Stalbridge who was said to possess the black art which she practised mainly on the cattle in the district. The villagers said that old Biddy put it in and Mother Herne of Milborne Down took it off.

Someone considering herself to be overlooked by Biddy consulted Mother Herne and was told, "There's a 'ooman at Stalbridge who's no good to 'ee. Look out for 'er, the fust 'ooman you d'meet on the way back."

Sure enough as Mother Herne's visitor was walking up Church Hill into the village whom should she meet but Old Biddy, her evil wisher.

There seemed to be something in the very air of Stalbridge which fostered this belief in the black art. A person still living in the village can remember seeing an old woman sitting by her fireside, stabbing pins into a bullock's heart, muttering and mumbling as she flung it into the fire.

Small wonder that bullocks' hearts have been found stuck in the chimneys of old Stalbridge houses, but strong as this belief was it has now completely died out. The villagers remember, but laugh away the stories of local witches. One story however persists concerning Mother Herne. It is said that after she lay dead in her cottage people came to look their last at the woman who by her strange power had helped them over their difficulties and ills. As if to show that even now she remained unconquered, legend has it that Mother Herne sat up in her coffin and spoke, but those mysterious words have never been recorded.

Author Olive Knott—she met Mother Herne

Wizard
of Sturminster Newton

"THIC MAN can make'ee believe the moon be a green cheese, or thic wheelbarrow a stage coach."

Such was the reputation earned by the cunning man at Piper's Corner on the top of Glue Hill, Sturminster Newton, and so true was the attribute that by various devices he had convinced most of the community in which he lived that he was possessed of magical powers.

When a farmer found that his sheep broke fold and strayed he would go to the wizard for help. "Cross me 'and with silver," the cunning man would say, "and you'll vind be marnin' the sheep be back in vold."

Sure enough the anxious farmer would find on his return that the sheep were all safe in the fold once more, but not for long because after a few days they would stray again and not until the farmer had paid another visit to the wizard could the sheep be induced to stay in the pen.

Sometimes the cunning man was sent for to help a farmer out of some difficulty and would have to pass through muddy fields to reach the farmhouse door.

Knowing full well there was no other way to reach the farm except through these muddy fields the farmer would note with astonishment that the wizard's boots were clean and polished with never a splash of mud.

Remarking upon them, the farmer was told, "I come high," so thus the cunning man earned the name of a fly-by-night and was included by the villagers in the band of broom-stick witches who rode the skies.

It was strange that no one wondered why the wizard carried on these expeditions a rush basket large enough to hold a pair of muddy boots!

There was no doubt about it that the cunning man lived by his wits, for no help would he give unless his hand was crossed by silver and never were sheep known to stray so often as in the vicinity of Piper's Corner. Farm implements too, and tools, would not infrequently be found missing and it was the incident of a pick being lost which eventually led to the unmasking of this artful old dodger.

A man discovered one morning that his pick had disappeared. Greatly perturbed he went to the cunning man who told him as usual to cross his hand with silver. "Now," said the wizard, "You must do exactly what I say. Goo t'bed as usual and be sure t'put out the light, and in the marnin' you'll vind yer pick back where you put'n."

This time fate was not on the side of the cunning man. It may have been his persistence in telling the other to go to bed as usual which awoke in the mind of the latter a definite suspicion. He put out the light as as commanded but he did not go to bed. He sat up the whole night long and watched from his bedroom window. Just as daylight was breaking who should hobble up to the shed with the missing pick in his hand, but the cunning man himself!

The man at the window, his suspicions confirmed, now livid with rage, shouted out, "You wold bugger! So 'twas thee, was it! Give I back my money!" His prestige now thoroughly undermined, the power of the cunning man gradually began to wane till only very few now ever crossed his hand with silver.

The old crone from Ansty

FAR FROM any towns, in the centre of the Dorset Downs, Hall and Woodhouse had a brewery in the remote hamlet of Ansty where a number of tracks converge from distant parts of the chalkland heights and from the Blackmore Vale below. Theirs was the one industry in the district and the brewery used to employ most of the local labour force which came from scattered farms and cottages. These people seldom had a break from country living and it was even rare to make the journey to a market town. So for this lonely upland community the firm's annual outing was considered the event of the year.

On one such occasion early in this century a party set out for Weymouth packed close together on the hard benches of horse-drawn wagons. After a twenty mile journey they arrived at Weymouth and all went well. The summer weather permitted bathing, paddling and all the delights of the side-shows along the front, but as the long day drew to its close, clouds began to gather and by the time the party assembled for the return journey the rain fell in torrents. There was a rush for the one wagon which was covered and a young woman in the company who had travelled down in one of the other conveyances took a seat in the covered wagon.

An old crone, whose seat she had taken, looked into the wagon and demanded her place. The girl, however, refused to give it up.

The old woman, then, shaking her fist at the girl, called out, "You mark my words, you won't get home tonight."

With that she withdrew and found a seat in one of the uncovered vehicles.

The wagon started off in the pouring rain. Those without cover reached home safely, despite the discomfort of rain trickling down the necks of the occupants who huddled beneath old sacks or coats or anything which could be found.

But, before the covered wagon had travelled very far a wheel came off and the unfortunate occupants, delayed by the search for someone to assist them, did not reach home till morning.

Susan Woodrow
of Turner's Puddle

REVEREND WILLIAM ETTRICK, an educated and unsuperstitious clergyman who was vicar of Affpuddle and Turner's Puddle at the beginning of the nineteenth century, suffered a series of misfortunes which completely converted his disbelief of the occult into a sincere fear of witchcraft. These misfortunes, occurring over a period of about a year, coincided with the arrival and presence of a particular servant at his vicarage in the tiny and lonely hamlet of Turner's Puddle on the edge of the heath near Bere Regis.

It took Mr. Ettrick a long time to come round to his eventual conviction that he was under an evil spell, but once he had, all seemed to confirm his suspicions. He kept a diary and recounted the curious and highly unpleasant events, all of which fit in with the movements of Susan Woodrow. She arrived at the house on 23 February, 1804, to work in the garden; she was renowned for her 'powers' with plants and vegetables, and Mr. Ettrick had employed her for that reason.

Four days after her arrival, Mr. Ettrick's horse—a young and healthy animal—fell sick. At this point he made no connection, though looking back later, he did. The horse apparently recovered.

Susan herself fell ill for a 'long time' and was away from the house until June. The day she came back, the same horse cut its foot and was lame for more than ten days. On 2 September, "the poor old horse caught a cold, and the Strangles." The animal worsened, catching other painful infections, until 16 September, when it died. Mr. Ettrick still did not suspect witchcraft and instead blamed the vet.

Four days later a pig was killed because it was ill. Mr. Ettrick now became suspicious. There was no apparent reason for the horse's sickness and death, nor that of the pig, and his dog had also died without cause. All medication to the animals had failed inexplicably. A horse he borrowed to fetch potatoes was also "very weak and seemingly going the way of mine by the vile witchcraft of a bad neighbour."

To add to his problems, all his children had fallen ill and the youngest was very ill indeed.

This youngest child, a boy, was born on 22 July, 1804. Susan Woodrow was at the house at the time and acted as nurse at the birth. She was the first to hold the new-born baby. From the moment of its birth, according to Mr. Ettrick, the child was in continual pain and torment. By November, after four months of constant anxiety and sleepless nights over his child, he connected this illness with the death of his horse. On 14 November, the day he borrowed his neighbour's horse, he writes: "I was once incredulous about the power of witchcraft, but have no doubts remaining." Of the child's illness, he writes: "It is like a demoniacal possession and began immediately after the child was snatched out of the mother's arms, by a hag reputed to be a witch."

This is the first indication that he suspected Susan. These suspicions continued and crystallised. He sent Susan away, and procured a phylactory which had been "inscribed with sacred words in the original character" and tied it round the child's body. The baby began to improve, and eventually seemed to have recovered completely.

But at the end of November, Susan returned to wash and perform various tasks. The child immediately sickened again. In his diary of 1 December, Mr. Ettrick directly accuses Susan Woodrow—according to him, she had often dropped expressions suggesting great pleasure at the child's sickness, and never once commiserated with its suffering or wished it better. Mr. Ettrick finally felt that as long as her connection with the house remained, they would be under her power.

He decided to dismiss her, but did not actually do so until January 1805—and he then dismissed her as much for her impudence and deceit as for her witchcraft, of which he had openly accused her, giving it merely as one of the reasons for her dismissal.

Three days before he sacked her, he had a dream in which a strange, gruesome, black bird flew into the parlour where he was sitting and flew around him several times. It then perched upon his hat and he seized the bird, and with great difficulty wrung its neck, and then threw it to the floor. The cat, which was in the room, though eyeing the bird with a cat's natural eagerness, would not approach it.

It had taken the vicar a month to pluck up the courage to confront Susan and send her away. The dream seemed to have exorcised her evil influence and given him the courage to act.

Susan Woodrow, however, did not give up immediately. Three days later, on 7 January, she reappeared at the house with two letters from a neighbour which she had offered to deliver, presumably, or at least in Mr. Ettrick's opinion, to regain admission to the house and procure a fresh power there. But Mr. Ettrick refused to accept the letters from her and instead threatened her with a warrant for her removal if she would not leave willingly. After demanding to know from Mr. Ettrick what it was she was supposed to have done, she eventually left, though with great reluctance.

There is no further mention in the diary of the child, nor of any other trouble. It seems that the child recovered and the family's misfortunes ceased. Mr. Ettrick never had enough substantial proof against her for any court charges—"her crime admits of no legal proofs, being all works of darkness." He does however list what he calls "The works of Susan" and it is for us to decide whether there was any witchcraft outside the paranoia of the vicar's own mind:

- the long and continued illness of the horse,
- the illness and death of a neighbour's horse,
- potatoes sorted by Susan and stored in the usual place were found rotten, whereas others less carefully stored were quite sound and good,
- the quarter of the garden dug by Susan had a succession of crop failures,
- the bees, which Susan had dealt with, had by the end of 1805 deserted their hives and left empty combs—Mr. Ettrick decided to keep no more bees.

The stylised Victorian idea of a witch, as
a crone on a broomstick. Many witches
believed they could fly. They sent their
minds on a 'trip' under the influence of
hallucinatory drugs.

Mary Ann Bull
at Shillingstone

THE NAME of Mary Ann Bull brings to the mind of those who remember her the picture of a ferocious old woman with stick in hand trudging beside her pony and cart, a man's hat crowning her weather-beaten face, a pair of man's boots encasing her feet.

Some will remember her, when in rare moments of repose, she sat by the roadside smoking cheap shag in a blackened clay pipe. At all times she drew curious stares from passers-by and noting this she would call out: "'Ave 'ee zeed all thee'se want t'zee? Mind thee eyes don't drop out!"

Mary Ann was a nomad and like the wandering tribes of the desert, carried wherever she went the whole of her worldly possessions. She hailed from a gipsy clan of north-east Dorset but like the proverbial rogue elephant had broken away from her kind and preferred to make her wide circuit alone.

She appeared with her merchandise—reddle for marking sheep and silver sand for cleaning harness—at regular intervals in the towns and villages of Somerset and Dorset.

When the clanging of the buckets and cans dangling from the axle of her cart heralded her approach the children of the neighbourhood would, from a safe distance, call out, "Mary Ann Bull! Mary Ann Bull!" till she began to flourish her stick and curse her tormentors or, more terrorizing still, let loose the snarling dog tied to the axle amongst the buckets and cans.

Folded like the Arab's, the old woman's inadequate tent reposed with her wares in her two-wheeled cart, ready to be set up wherever its owner's fancy led her to camp for the night. For Mary Ann Bull had no caravan to give her shelter and no tumble-down cottage to call her home.

Although more often than not she was heard to curse and to swear, she could on occasion be civil and although she would, if possible, strike her tormentors, she was kind to the pony she had owned for so long.

When the pony died the folks at a Dorset village collected enough to buy her another. This was done not for love of Mary Ann—but in order to break the spell she was believed to cast upon those she chose to ruin.

Quite frequently the old woman would, by means of a mug of ale, escape from her loveless life into a realm, where maybe, she reigned as Gipsy Queen or dwelt in a painted caravan down some shady lane. Many a time she was in the hands of the police for her bouts of drunkenness, but nothing daunted, she would drink again when opportunity arose.

It was in connection with this weakness of Mary Ann's that she employed her black art. One day on her rounds at Shillingstone, she demanded a drink from one of the villagers. The request was refused, however, and in a fit of temper Mary Ann turned to a young woman of the company telling her that bad luck would follow her wherever she went.

Strangely enough, ill-luck dogged the footsteps of the girl. Shortly after her marriage her husband died and nothing she undertook seemed to prosper.

It was, too, in connection with Mary Ann's inordinate love of drinking that death came to this lone traveller of the roads. She was found frozen to death, beneath her cart by the side of the road, near Yeovil. She had never awakened from a drunken sleep.

The inquest over her body was held at Wincanton, and this lonely old woman who had broken away from her clan could not claim the distinction of a gipsy funeral, but was buried with scant ceremony at public expense among the dead whom during her lifetime she had never known.

Mummified Cat
at Blandford

THE DISCOVERY in May 1963 of the mummified body of
a cat sealed in the wall of a cottage being demolished
at Blandford started speculation that the animal might
have been a witch's familiar or have been involved in
some ritual sacrifice. It was found standing on a ledge
about six feet from the floor, sandwiched between a
lath-and-plaster partition and a brick wall. Only a few
inches away was a volume of prose and poetry published
in 1851.

This was entitled "The Speaker," with the explana-
tion that it contained "miscellaneous pieces selected
from the best English writers, with a view to facilitating
the improvement of youth in reading and speaking."
Inside the cover was an inscription: "John Chaffey, from
his sincere friend and well-wisher, James Hunt, 3 Victoria Terrace, Swanage, Oct. 12/63."

Said Mr. Jack Raymond, of Milton Abbas, who
demolished the building: "The wall was completely
plastered up, and there was no sign of any opening, so
I don't see how the cat could have got in there by
accident. The book was bound in black, and someone
who saw it suggested that somebody, unable to read or
write, might have placed it beside the body of the cat
thinking it was a Bible."

The cottage was number six, Whitecliff Mill Street,
and now lies under part of Fiander's garage. Mrs. Grace
James, wife of the newsagent at the Plocks, told a
reporter the building had been the home of her family
shop there.

The point that cats do sometimes come to a natural
end inside cavity walls, through their own curiosity,
was made in a letter to a local newspaper a couple of
weeks later. Mr. R. G. Tapper wrote that when No. 51
Durweston was being repaired by estate workmen in
1903 they found the mummified body of a ginger cat:
"It was in a good state of preservation, completely flat.
Claws and the whiskers were in perfect condition. I

showed the body to the late William Green, who lived there previously, and he identified it as a cat he had lost many years before. He also remembered that at the time the cat was missing, the wall was being repaired, and the cavity was left open overnight. The workmen finished bricking up the hole the next morning, unaware that the cat was inside."

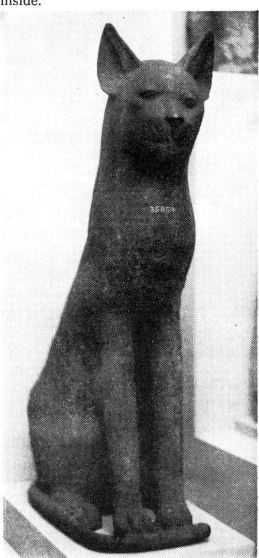

The Egyptians frequently mummified their cats. This carving, from one of the great tombs in the desert, is in the British Museum.

Mother Burt
of East Knighton

SOMETIMES AN instance of poltergeist activity became confused with witchcraft. Half-way through the last century, in one of the cob and thatch cottages on the wild heathland at East Knighton, near Wool, there lived Mrs. Kerley with her daughter who was about eighteen.

The daughter was supposed to have been bewitched and the subject of strange manifestations. Villagers positively declared that articles were thrown out of the cottage into the street, although neither the window nor the door was open, and they said that these were sent flying in all directions.

This is a typical poltergeist description, fitting the standard form as it involves a young girl, but the villagers looked to witchcraft as the cause. An old woman, named Burt, was blamed for all the mischief, particularly as she was once supposed to have changed into a hare and been chased by the neighbours—and then to have sat up, as hares do, and looked defiantly at them.

Everyone firmly believed that until blood was drawn from Mother Burt the manifestations would not cease. We do not know what happened to this almost certainly harmless if ageing lady, but at East Knighton more than anywhere in Dorset it is now difficult to visualise how the powers of darkness and witchcraft could have reigned supreme almost into living memory. Today the humble mud-walled homes of the old heath-cropping community are dwarfed beside the steaming nuclear reactors of Winfrith's atomic energy establishment. Equally, there has come a divide between the minds of this century and last, and at least any modern Mother Burt would be spared persecution that lacked all subtlety.

Jinny Gould
of Ulwell

THE HAMLET of Ulwell lies at the south foot of Ballard Down, Swanage, beside a gap in the ridge of the Purbeck Hills through which the road runs to Studland. There once stood an old toll gate and in the cottage near by dwelt a witch known as Jinny Gould.

Jinny and the toll gate had always been associated and long after Jinny passed away the gate was said to have opened of its own accord to allow lonely midnight travellers to pass through. For this reason the villagers called it 'Jinny Ghoul Gate'.

The best-known story about Jinny Gould is told by an old carrier who says that late one night he was returning home after his nightly visit to the local, where he had drunk rather too freely of home-brewed ale, when as he approached the Ulwell Gate, he saw, etched against the sky, the figure of an enormous black cat, sitting on top of it.

There was something about the way in which the cat sat with its motionless stare which sent a shiver down the spine of the lonely traveller.

Suddenly with a drunken yell, he lifted his whip and struck the cat a heavy blow across its back.

Strange to relate the cat disappeared—that is, it vanished into thin air!

Next day old Jinny Gould was found dead in her cottage by the toll gate, with a great wound across her back.

Around 1896, a young boy called Walter Steer was taken by his nurse to Ulwell, and he wandered into a plot of ground which contained a few ruined walls and the faint traces of a garden. He wanted to pick a rose, but his nurse hauled him out and shook him, telling him that if he went there again he would be spanked as it was a 'wicked place.' He had apparently found his way into Jinny Gould's territory.

Witch-hare
of Worth Matravers

WORTH MATRAVERS makes its contribution to Dorset witch-lore in the shape of a large hare, which on account of its unusual size became the target of many a hunter, but no shot could reach the elusive creature. Although so large, it was noticeably agile and bounded away from its pursuers with incredible swiftness.

Many a villager returning home from work would spot the hare in the distance and take aim, but to no avail.

"I zid'n again," said a labourer to his wife after an unsuccessful shot, "but do'ee think I could get'n, not I."

"You mark my words," his wife replied, "'tis a witch, an' on'y a silver sixpence behind thic charge'll get rid o' she."

With these words the woman fetched a little wooden box in which she kept a hoard of coins and after a good deal of rattling about produced the necessary coin. She handed it to her husband saying: "Put he behind yer charge, an' thic hare'll be a gonner."

Obediently the man did as his wife advised and when next he saw the monstrous hare he shot it in the leg.

The death of the hare proved the means of revealing which of the suspected old women of the village was a witch, for, from the day on which the hare was shot a certain old woman suddenly became a cripple.

Devil's bush
at Langton

THOUGH THE Purbeck parish of Langton Matravers is lacking in stories of witchcraft, a lonely gorse bush, on the outskirts of the village below the quarrymen's hamlet of Acton, was once the focus of supernatural fear and has ever since been known as the Devil's Bush.

There is nothing to distinguish this bush from any other unless it is the fact of its obvious age.

Maybe, there existed in the minds of the simple village folk a sharp contrast between the might of God and the dark power of evil, associated with witchcraft.

Well versed as they were in the scriptures, they would be acquainted with the story of the burning bush, from which the voice of God pronounced the spot as holy ground. It is easy to assume that seeing the perpetual bloom of the golden gorse, they were awed by this phenomenon of nature. Then, perhaps one or two accidents occurred in the vicinity of the bush, or some misfortune befell a traveller near the gorse on the lonely road. This would be enough to arouse a fear which became centred around the mysterious bush blooming throughout the year, a fear so strong that it came to be regarded as Satan incarnate and was christened the Devil's Bush.

That woman of Church Knowle

THE FOLLOWING story was told by an old ex-poacher living at Church Knowle, near Corfe Castle; it was related to him by a friend who lived in the days of horses and carts.

One day this friend was taking a heavy load into Corfe with his aged mother also seated in the cart. When they had reached about halfway they overtook an old woman whom, as they drew nearer, they recognized as she who was known as the Witch of Church Knowle.

The old woman called out, asking for a lift into Corfe. The driver, however, whipped up his horse and made to drive past her. But when the horse drew level with the woman, she turned and spoke to the animal which immediately became rooted to the spot. Neither whip, nor oath, nor exhortation would induce the horse to move.

The man had no other option but to walk backwards and forwards carrying the load bit by bit to its destination, his old mother hobbling as best she might by the side of the road.

Help came eventually, however, in the shape of the witch herself, for presently she was seen on her return journey from Corfe. When she reached the horse the spell was removed. Unmolested, the man's mother mounted the cart, and the journey to Corfe was made without incident.

Maria Gover, the Purbeck hare

THE SAME OLD poacher at Church Knowle tells another witch story which has similarities with the tales of Mother Weller at Milborne Port and, in Purbeck itself, Jinny Gould of Ulwell.

Our informant's father had one day been out with his old 'granfer' doing a little poaching. Suddenly granfer espied a large hare lying in the grass. Quick as thought he lifted his stout stick and dealt the hare a heavy blow behind the ears. To the amazement of the two onlookers the hare bounded across the field and disappeared into the garden surrounding the cottage of old Maria Gover who had the reputation of being a witch.

Next day, the news went around the village that old Maria had been taken to bed, and within a day or two she was dead.

Lost dog of West Moors

BRANDY, the roan and white sheep-dog with the appealing brown eyes, was lost. There was a hue and cry all over the farm which was his home and his young mistress was almost in tears. A well-known figure in West Moors, a Polish count, happened to call that day at the farm, and learning of the disaster, suggested phoning a woman at Bournemouth who was considered to possess occult powers and who, twenty years before this, would have been termed a witch.

"My friend is in trouble," said the count over the phone. The reply came; "You are in trouble. Your friend is in trouble. She has lost her dog." Then the voice described the sheep-dog in every detail, even to the sadness of his eyes. "The dog will travel far afield," the voice continued, "but you will find him, quite well, tied to a caravan."

Strangely enough, so convincing was this message that Brandy's mistress experienced a feeling of certainty that her dog would be found.

Eighteen months passed by, during which time there was neither sight nor sound of Brandy. Till, one morning; a very dirty-looking animal bolted on to the lawn, snatched up the ball which had lain there untouched for so long, rushed wildly into the house and laid it at the feet of the farmer's young wife. Then, leaping and barking, he licked her face, hands and every available part of her body.

It was Brandy, but a very dirty Brandy although, as the voice foretold, in good condition. Later, it was discovered that his lower teeth had been filed (evidently for rabbit catching) and his ears pierced for reasons unknown.

When, with a beaming countenance, the cow-man appeared at the kitchen door, he related how he had seen Brandy that morning half a mile away, tied to the wheel of a gipsy's caravan. He had gone immediately and released him with the foregoing happy result.

It was not until later, information casually picked up in the 'local' from one and another of the gipsy tribe, revealed that Brandy had been enticed from his home by a gipsy with aniseed. He had travelled as far as Sussex with the gipsies who had stolen him and then having changed hands, he had come with another tribe back to the Isle of Wight. Evidently he had been well-fed and not unkindly treated. No doubt with his blunted teeth he had laid many a rabbit at the feet of his unlawful owners.

Brandy had apparently changed hands several times during the eighteen months he was away, his last captor bringing him to within half a mile of his own home.

It was here that the cowman had sighted him, resigned apparently to his fate, but only when released did it become apparent that Brandy had not forgotten and beneath his shaggy dirty coat his faithful heart was transported with joy at the prospect of home once more.

Spell failure
near Poole

A MODERN verstion of the waxen image superstition was
told a few years ago by an aged Dorset woman living
near Poole, relating how she herself once tried to work
an evil spell upon her brother-in-law whom she hated
with a bitter hatred.

What he had done so wrong she would not say.

The woman said that she had gone to his mother
who possessed a photograph of her son, and asked if
she could buy it. His mother, however, gave her the
photo, saying "What do'ee want'n for?"

"I'll show 'ee what I want'n for," the girl replied
and so saying took the photo from the woman's hands
cut off the ears, nose and mouth of the man she hated.
She then hung what was left of the photo on to a tree
by her window and, like those who christened the waxen
image centuries before, she prayed to God that her
brother-in-law would die like a dog in a ditch.

On being asked if she had heard of wax figures the
woman replied: "You d'mean taller (tallow). Oh, ah,
I've a'heard my gran'mother talk about taller, but I
thought a photo 'ud be better."

It does, perhaps, from the woman's point of view,
rather detract from the story, to say that the man in
question, instead of pining away, flourished like the
proverbial green bay-tree.

Mother Shipton
of Corfe Mullen

THE MOST up-to-date contribution to these pages comes
from Corfe Mullen near Wimborne. Several people there
remember Mother Shipton, a supposed witch whose
notoriety was widespread, but they cannot call to mind
any particular story about her.

However, a young couple living at Corfe Mullen
in the 1950s were firmly convinced that their television
set was bewitched, as regularly every Saturday
evening, it would break down immediately the husband's
favourite jazz programme was due to begin.

Index